PERSPECTIVES

30 Days to a New Life
Through a New Lens

*Here's to
continually expanding
our perspectives.*

Charity Haderlie

CHARITY HADERLIE

ABOUT THE AUTHOR

Charity Haderlie helps people live true to their dreams instead of true to their fears through Success & Empowerment Coaching, keynoting & published works.

She also runs an annual personal development & growth mindset event, which has been changing lives, since she started in 2018.

In two words, Charity transforms cultures; whether it be the culture of the mind or the culture of the team, to help people become more connected and empowered, both personally and professionally.

From stage fright, social anxiety and severe depression to an accomplished speaker and published author, she is living her story of becoming more empowered.

When Charity takes her business hat off, she can be found enjoying the outdoors (the hammock between the trees is her happy place), playing volleyball (contrary to popular belief, white girls CAN jump! But Charity, not so much), learning about different cultures, tasting ethnic foods and attempting to recreate them at home.

She also enjoys a good round of karaoke and especially loves being with her favorite people in the whole world, her husband, Michael (married 21 years, baby!) and their four children ages 9-19.

Charity is happily available for keynotes, workshops, expert series and interviews.

Connect with Charity at CharityHaderlie.Com or Linktr.ee/CharityHaderlie for more resources.

ACKNOWLEDGEMENTS

They say it takes a village to raise a child, but did you know it also takes a village to write a book? To each of you who are part of my village: thank you from the bottom of my heart! I've listed several key players, but there are many more!

To my husband, Michael, for your encouragement to dream big and go for it, for being a constant source of strength, support and unconditional love. And to our four amazing children, for being my cheerleaders and dreaming with me, whether you get soup or cereal for dinner. Each of you mean the world to me!

To my parents, Tralena & Mike, who love me and gave me everything I needed to become who I am today. The journey just keeps getting better. Thank you for the foundation of grit, determination and faith.

To my siblings, all 10 of them! Jeremy, our guardian angel in Heaven, and the rest on earth who keep pushing me forward, but who also keep me humble and connected to my roots.

To my inlaws, for taking me in as your own daughter, sister and friend. Thank you loving me at every point in my messy journey, and for raising the man I married. He's the exactly who I need by my side.

To Veronica Walker, my friend in New Orleans who took me under her wing, nurtured me and mothered me, and who invited me to a seminar on mental health; which became a pivotal moment in my life.

To RexAnne Nielson, who saw something in me that I didn't see in myself. Your invitation (arm-twisting) to share my stories with your women's group years ago, awakened something in me that told me this is my path and I need to keep going.

To Tana Madison, my cheerleader, advisor and dear friend, who never lets me quit and who keeps me accountable.

To Fahim Rahim, my mentor, my friend and my brother; who has a passion for his purpose and a heart for humanity and who inspires me to keep dreaming big because those dreams create positive impact on the world.

To Ryan Harris, my friend and business associate, whose ideas are just as crazy as mine and who reminds me that we can totally tackle the impossible.

To Drew Brazier, my business coach, friend and mentor who keeps me focused and on track, especially when I face roadblocks or I overwhelm myself with too many ideas to pursue.

To Dale Darley, my book branding mentor, friend and cheerleader.

To my church family, who has been a constant source of strength and friendship.

To my Toastmasters family, who cheered me on and helped me refine and grow my presentation skills even before I saw myself as a public speaker.

Most importantly, to my higher power, who is guiding my steps and expanding my comfort zone. I am your perfectly imperfect servant who is willing to simply say yes to what feels impossible and then ask for and expect your help. I did not begin this journey with the ability, but I am willing to learn along the way.

This book has taken a life filled with experiences, both healthy and unhealthy, to open my own perspective so that I could learn how to create a new life, through a new lens. A journey that will continue through out a lifetime.

DEDICATION

Y ou, dear reader, are the reason I wrote this book.

Although we may not have met, yet, I trust we are more alike than you may think.

Has doubt ever derailed your dreams? Has fear frozen you in your footsteps? You know what it's like to turn away from a goal because it feels too big, or you think your impact and capacity are too small to make a difference, don't you? Yeah, me too.

But this book isn't about dwelling on those fears or setbacks; it's about transforming the very culture of the mind. See, culture did not exist for any of us, the day we were born. It's learned and developed over time.

Imagine a young child full of life and exciting dreams. Inside a small body was a big spirit, bursting with energy and ideas.

Over time, experiences in life unwittingly wove negativity and criticism into this child's mind without her even realizing. Ever so subtly, the external critics became her internal critics, and she began looking through a lens of doubt, fear, judgment, anger, etc.

One by one these "negative lenses" clouded her vision, blocking out the light and love that existed around her. Eventually, she stopped hoping and dreaming. She even stopped believing in herself.

That child was me. Does that child sound like you, too? It's easy to forget we have everything we need inside to create the life we want. And you are about to discover the steps I took to get from surviving to thriving, from destroying myself with a toxic mindset to creating a new life, through a new lens. I went from being alive to living, and feeling connected to who I am deep inside and how I'm meant to help others do the same.

Perhaps you've felt stuck, as well, when you wanted to grow and move forward. Perhaps you've also felt you don't measure up or aren't good enough. Know that you're not alone in that feeling. Many of us struggle in similar ways, but often we are quietly, almost imperceptibly, comparing someone else's strengths to our own weaknesses, or reacting to subtle thoughts we don't even notice. Each thought we experience, whether we notice it or not, creates a feeling and that feeling puts us on a pathway which can default to a reactionary pathway rather than one we choose with intention.

The purpose of this book is to help you become more aware of whether your thoughts are lifting you up or tearing you down, and whether they are leading you to action or inaction. As you work through this book, you'll find doubt evaporating into empowerment, and that will transform fear into action. You'll also be learn how to kick that perfectionist mentality to the curb.

Are you ready?
Let's dive in!

CONTENTS

WHAT YOU'LL FIND IN THIS BOOK

Section I:

This section includes "Inspect Your Perspective," a personal assessment which will do just what it says! Ugh! I know, I know. But stay with me, there's a saying that goes: "You can't improve what you don't measure", so if you sincerely want to transform your mindset and measure your results, then the quiz is a vital tool to measure your progress. Take it before you begin on day 1, and repeat again after you finish the book so you can track your progress.

Disclaimer: if you end up with minimal progress, consider your efforts. Were they also minimal? Or were you all in? You'll get out of this book what you put into it. As your perspective shifts, you'll rediscover the awesomeness that is in you! Your confidence and intuition will begin to flourish and you will discover endless possibilities and increased capacity within yourself. Be careful, though, because it can totally change your life! :)

Section II:

This section is where you'll journey with me, as I tell you some stories from my own life and how I discovered 3 simple, yet powerful steps, which are the core of this process. Each step has become foundational in my life. By implementing them, I've overcome and championed my own toxic mindset, which had dragged me into the depths of depression. After testing them out, I also discovered they aren't just for overcoming negatives, but also for connecting to your purpose and to your passion, and for accomplishing big dreams and goals you never thought possible!

They are tried and true and everything I am building in my life is a result of implementing these 3 steps daily! They took me many painful years to discover and develop, and I am honored to share them with you in just 30 days! If you do the work, I promise you will reap rewards for years to come.

Section III:

This section is divided by days. Each day has one original quote from a list I've been compiling over the years. They've been waiting for just the right moment to be shared with you. They are designed to provoke thought, shift perspective, and help you see things through a new lens.

Along with each daily quote, you'll find questions and simple action steps. Again, the effort you put into this is up to you, and the reward will match your efforts. Take

5-10 minutes each morning and evening to ponder and answer the questions, and then be sure to get to work during the day with those actions.

You have ideas and goals for a reason. You have an important purpose. You can create a positive impact. You have exactly what you need inside. Come on, my friend, I'll guide you each step of the way. Let's go!

Section IV:
This section houses the "Inspect Your Perspective" personal assessment once again. Set aside some quiet time to complete and then compare your results between the two assessments.

SECTION I:
INSPECT YOUR PERSPECTIVES

Let's begin! First thing's first. You knew it was coming and it's time to dive in! Find a quiet place where you can sit and go through the assessment. Jot down the first number that comes to mind in the "where I am column" and also in the "where I want to be column". There are no right or wrong answers, just notice where you are and where you want to be.

Shifting perspectives can only come through self-awareness, so don't cheat yourself out of taking the quiz both before and after the 30 days. Remember, you can't improve what you don't measure and this is an excellent way to measure.

The tools you'll learn are not a "temporary fix", nor are they "one and done." They are tools you can use daily, not just to strengthen your ability and resolve to champion your thoughts, but also to help you move toward your goals and toward discovering your passion and purpose!

Inspect Your Perspective

Where I am Now   **Where I Want to Be**

0-10	STATEMENT	0-10
	I recognize my emotions as I feel them	
	I can identify when what I'm feeling is a result of what I'm thinking or saying to myself	
	I recognize how my internal dialogue influences the way I feel	
	I feel that I can truly be myself around others	
	I notice whether things are happening to me or within me	
	I recognize the consequences of my thoughts and internal dialog	
	I am an active listener when others speak to me	
	I keep my emotions in check and choose to act instead of react	

	I can easily build rapport with others	
	I can read other's emotions	
	I know how to calm myself down when I feel upset or anxious	
	I invite feedback and ways to improve	
	I pay attention to what my heart and mind are nudging me to do	
	I set long term goals and assess them on a regular basis	
	I am confident in making decisions and taking action on them	
	I feel strong and capable	
	I know how to calm myself when I'm upset and I don't let it derail my whole day	
	I know I have weaknesses and I'm not embarrassed by them	

	I am aware of how I spend my time each day	
	I am aware of my habits	
	I am aware of my expectations	
	I'm aware of how I respond when expectations aren't met	
	I don't expect others to live up to my unspoken expectations, I love them where they are	
	I plan time for fun and relaxation	
	I allow time for reflection in my day	
	I take action daily toward my goals	
	I focus on the lessons in life rather than the losses	
	I keep my emotions in check and don't let them derail my day or week	

	I love myself	
	The words I say to myself are kind, forgiving and loving	
	I don't avoid conflict, I face challenges and look for ways beyond them	
	←Add each number down the columns and write your answers→	

SECTION II:
INTRO TO
MY STORY

CHAPTER 1:
IN OVER MY HEAD

Life is not about perfection. It's about progression. It's about standing up one more time than you fall, especially when you feel like you're in over your head.

Do you remember playing in a kiddie pool as a child? I was about 7-years-old and my two older brothers and I were in our backyard, next to the mulberry tree. We ran around the edges of the pool until the water was swirling as fast as we were. I sat on a float, feet dangling on either side in the cool water, as the sun warmed my back. The water whisked me around, then one of my brothers swam underneath me. Just before he was out from under my float, he stood up and I flipped backward, into the pool. My nose burned as water gushed inside and I panicked! I didn't know how to swim! That 2 ½ feet of water, instantly felt like a bottomless pit!

I flailed and thrashed about for something or someone to pull me out of the water! But I felt nothing. I was *sure* I was going to drown that day. And then, a simple thought came to me: "Stand up." I dismissed it because I thought I was already doing everything I could to get out of the water. How could I just *stand up*? Again, the thought gently nudged me once again.

As soon as I leaned forward in the motion to stand, my feet hit solid ground, and I rose out of the water. I coughed and gasped for air and then I sobbed. I am forever grateful that I listened to such a simple thought that came to me that day I thought I was going to drown.

CHAPTER 2:
3 TRANSFORMATIONAL STEPS

Have you ever felt like you were drowning? Each time we get our heads above water, and rise above our struggles, we come out with lessons learned. What I discovered over time, were 3 simple, yet powerful steps that have become foundational in my own life, and I'm excited to share them with you!

Have you ever worn a pair of eclipse glasses? Through these dark lenses, the brilliant and blazing sun in the sky is reduced to a tiny dot in the distance. Sometimes in life we look at ourselves through a negative lens of doubt, fear, judgment, etc. When we do this, we feel small, fearful, doubtful, less important, less impactful, less capable, less needed, less worthy, less loved.

When I was in my early twenties, I found myself drowning once again. This time-depression (more on that in chapter 3). As I look back on the pattern of my life, I realize that over and over again, when I focused on what I lacked and the mistakes I made, I was blinded from what I still had the power to control. Now, I recognize that the lens through which I view myself is something I can choose. So this brings us to the first step in this process of transforming the culture of the mind.

Step # 1: Change Your Lens

On that summer day as a young girl, I had the power the whole time to stand up, yet because I focused on my lack of swimming skills, I reacted in fear. As I was thrashing around in panic mode, I was the only one keeping myself under water. Many people keep themselves "under water" as they live life reacting to what's going on around them, rather than choosing how they will respond. Has that ever happened to you?

Over time, l learned to change my lens from negative to positive, over and over again. It's a daily choice that increases our confidence, energy, and momentum to rise above struggles. So, instead of letting shortcomings and fear become the focus, consider changing your lens. I'll walk you through exactly what this means and how to do it in the next section, but let's move on to the second step.

Step #2: LISTen

That summer day in the pool, when the thought came to me to stand up, I dismissed it because it seemed too simple. I had already done everything I thought I could to get out from under water, yet because I listened, my life was saved.

Notice LIST is emphasized. List those nudges that pull at your heartstrings or bring your mind a flash of clarity. Once they are written, either do them right away or add them to your calendar with a specific time slot. That way you'll be sure to get it done.

It may be a simple thought that comes to you, but those ones that you want to dismiss or wrestle with, are just what you need when you're in over your head.

As I look back on my years of battling depression, I realize that I had been listening, but not to the positive forces in the world. Since I had been looking through a lens of doubt and fear, etc, I had allowed the external critics to become my internal critic. What I would LIST in my mind were my flaws and failures which only dragged myself down once again. But here's the point— we always have a choice with what we think and how we think, but we have to be aware of it before we can do anything to change it. Speaking of change, the third step is where all the magic and transformation expand exponentially. It is also THE MOST DIFFICULT for everyone of us. Are you ready for this?

Step # 3: Take Action

On that summer day, taking action made all the difference! I found that I already had the power to stand up, even though I doubted its simplicity. There is power in taking action. As soon as I began the motion to stand up, my feet hit solid ground, and I was able to rise out of the water. In the very moment we begin to take action, we recognize we aren't in as deep as we thought. Knowledge is power, but action is empowering. It is how we expand our comfort zones, and how we find lasting and sustainable results. The power is in the daily action we take.

I'll remind you that this is the most difficult part for many of us. We can often choose to change our lens, and then LISTen to what's pulling at the heart and mind and write it on our calendar, but when we begin to make a move, we are instantly filled with fear and doubt all over again. Has that ever happened to you? Have you ever felt stuck? What does one do?

Go back again to change your lens. Negative feelings clue you in to which lens you're looking through. Choose to look through a lens of belief that you have this nudge at your heart for a reason, and you must trust that taking this action will help you learn something. When we focus on learning instead of performing, then taking action becomes less scary and risky. We don't have anything to lose if we focus on learning. Failure doesn't really exist when we focus on the task that can be done and the lesson to be learned.

Much like a flashlight in the darkness—we can only see so far onto the pathway, it's only when we take a step that we can discover the next step, and then the next and the next.

Don't worry, I'll guide you through this every day in the next section.

CHAPTER 3:
PERFECTLY IMPERFECT

Now it gets even more personal. In my early 20's, my husband and I moved to New Orleans, LA, to embark upon a new adventure. He was pursuing more schooling and training and we had a darling little boy who was 18 months old. Our little car was stuffed with our belongings, and we were about 2000 miles away from our friends and family and everything that we knew and loved.

Once again, I found myself drowning. This time-depression. Depression is an unpredictable disorder. Things can be going well in your life, as they were for me and my family at that time, and then past experiences and emotions we thought were tucked away in a vault, can break or leak through the surface and drag us down.

I didn't realize I had depression; it didn't match the stereotype. Even though I was good at pretending to be happy and kindly blending in with the crowd, I felt alone—as though I were seeing my own life through the eyes of a stranger. I was disconnected from myself and from those around me, even those close to me. I had felt that way for as long as I could remember, but it seemed to be getting worse.

One day, a new friend invited me to a seminar. She told me how great and engaging the speaker was; plus there's free babysitting, so I went with her. When I found out the topic was depression, I wanted out, but she was my ride, so I stayed.

At one point, the presenter, a psychologist, passed out an assessment to gauge our levels of anxiety/depression. On a scale of 0 to about 65, my score indicated that I had severe depression. I got a 48!

Depression? I couldn't believe it. I didn't want to believe it. I acted as though it were no big deal. Just kept my cool and I thought I'd prove this assessment wrong. So I took an extra copy home to my husband. He humored me and then showed me his score. I told him, "No, no, you need to turn it around and do both sides, then add them together." He said, "I did, I got a 5. . . what did you get?"

It was like a pile of bricks hit my stomach. I stood there frozen in shock because I was both too prideful and too embarrassed to admit I had a serious problem! As the realization settled in that he was still awaiting my answer, I crumpled up the assessment and said, "Oh, never mind. It's just a dumb quiz anyway." Then I hurried down the hall to my bedroom, as my emotions burst to the surface and cascaded down my cheeks.

After a short time of stewing over this new piece of painful information, I called my older brother, who had also battled depression. I told him about the assessment and mentioned how this wall of depression had gradually been thickening like a dark fog—draining my energy and sucking the life out of me. It was getting worse.

Amid this dark cloud, however, there was a silver lining. That silver lining was that for as long as I could remember, I often felt that I was defective. I felt like a faker no matter who I talked to or what I did. I often wondered if my husband would someday find out that I was defective, too, and then what would he do? Would he still accept and love me? I was afraid to find out and so I carefully guarded my words and my actions, just in case.

You see, on the outside, I was positive, kind, and witty, but on the inside, I was destroying myself with the toxic culture of my mind.

I didn't realize that I had a choice in how to treat myself or what to say to myself. I was the one making myself feel defective, just as I was the one keeping myself under the water in the kiddie pool as a young child. It's not past experiences, critics or my flaws that made me feel this way—it was how I thought about past experiences, flaws, mistakes and so forth, that created a life filled with fear, doubt, hate, and hopelessness.

What I came to realize is that I am that I was the only one responsible for loving myself, for believing in myself, for being kind to myself. Recognizing that I could and need to treat myself with love and forgiveness, even more than I need to do that for a friend, has made all the difference. Many people do not realize they talk trash about themselves all day long in their own heads, and then wonder why they can't get that job, or a date or accomplish their goals.

The day I took that assessment was the first day of my journey to becoming whole again. To connecting my body-which is flawed and scared and lazy, and fearful; with my soul-which is beautiful and perfect and divine and inspired and fearless. Finally, I have learned how to take the trash out of my head in order to quiet fears and move forward in faith. I also learned to believe that I have ideas and dreams for a reason, and that my higher power doesn't need me to be able, He only needs me to be willing.

I will never be capable enough to do what He asks me to do, but if I am willing, He will magnify my weak offering of time, energy and talent, to become what He wants me to become. It's not about me. It's never been about me. It's not about proving myself **to** others; it's about improving myself **for** others. But I'm getting ahead of myself.

In that moment of awakening, I knew others had overcome depression, and that gave me hope that *maybe* I could, too. All this time I had thought I was defective, I had a mindset that was afraid of failure, afraid others might see my mistakes and weaknesses, afraid of success, afraid of being seen and heard. I was afraid to be myself. I wasn't comfortable in my own skin. In a word; I was afraid to be human.

Think about it! To be human is to err, so why are we so afraid of making mistakes? Does that mean we are afraid to be human? I used to think our purpose in life was to avoid mistakes and do everything right the first time. That's not so much to ask, is it? Well, it is if you're a human! And last time I checked, I am a perfectly imperfect human, who doesn't have it all figured out, who falls flat on my face, but I keep standing up. What about you—human too? Yep. We only have imperfect people to work with, including ourselves, so let's see what we can do to lift and help each other by connecting, rather than convincing. We truly need each other!

These are not things I realized over night, it took many years of learning and studying. I dove into psychology and matters of the mind and heart. I read personal development and performance books, topics on mental health, cognitive behavioral therapy, and so much more. I wanted to learn everything I could about depression, how the brain works, and if there were any way to break through this wall that had been holding me back. It was the first time I realized that maybe, just maybe, there was something I could do differently. Some way to come back to feeling like me.

CHAPTER 4: WHY POSITIVE AFFIRMATIONS DIDN'T WORK FOR ME

Have you used positive affirmations? I know many people who use them and they say they work for them, however, I don't teach my clients to use them. They didn't work for me. As often as I said, "I am beautiful" or "I am smart/capable" etc., I still didn't believe it. I felt fake saying them and my core belief system rejected them.

What I learned instead, is to harness the power of choice. The brain will look for evidence of whatever we believe–it is an expert detective! Making a choice bypasses negative subconscious programming, or core beliefs, and it gives our brains new evidence to look for.

So instead of saying "I am enough," I learned to say, "I choose to believe that I am enough" or instead of "I love myself," I would say, "I choose to look through a lens of love for myself" then I'd reach out to my higher power and plea for Him to help me love myself, or to look through a lens of faith and belief. I am not always capable of following through with the choice I make, but He is and when I take action anyway, He empowers me every single time.

Eventually, our choices rewire our internal programming and now I can honestly say that I do love myself, I do feel cabable and brave (most days), but the key here is just to be willing to take one step each day, even when I'm afraid.

I also believe that we are made of flesh and spirit. Our spirit is divine, whole, capable, and complete. Our physical bodies are lazy, flawed, selfish, and full of excuses. When we have a nudge pull at our hearts, our higher power has just spoken to our spirit, but then the human flesh begins to derail and ignore and fight that inspiration. The best way to connect our human body to our spirit, is to follow through with those nudges that come to our heart and our minds. The more we take action on them, the more our energy, capacity and creativity grows and expands. The only limit is when we doubt and turn away and keep ourselves down.

You don't have to know everything, just the next step. And when you take it, you'll find the next and the next. You'll find new opportunities and pathways that you never knew existed. And I promise you that your life experience is preparing you for what is next. You have what it takes! You have everything you need inside.

These 3 simple, yet powerful steps, will change you in ways you hadn't planned. They will move the mountains that hold you back, or lead you to a secret passageway to a world of other wonderful possibilities that are waiting just for you! These steps have worked for me. I am confident that they will work for you, too!

CHAPTER 5:
I COULDN'T SEE THE
CHANGES IN ME

About a year after I began my journey of overcoming, I was visiting the friend who had dragged me to the women's seminar. I had said nothing to her about having depression. She looked at me funny, then asked, 'Charity, are you pregnant?" So, of course, I sucked in my gut and said, "No, I am not pregnant. Why would you ask that?" She said, "There's just something about you. . . the only way I can describe it is the pregnancy glow. Are you sure you're not pregnant?" I assured her I was not pregnant, but of course I went home and took a pregnancy test, just in case.

As I pondered why she had asked what she did, I recognized that the more I trusted in this process, the less I felt like a stranger in my own body. I was becoming connected to myself, and also to those around me but, more importantly, I was becoming more connected to my higher power. I was not just surviving and going through the motions of life, I was beginning to thrive! It was igniting something in my soul that has grown over the years. as I have continued to implement these 3 simple steps.

Feeling connected to the process of learning and loving myself, even when I fall, has been a life-changer. Remember that failure is merely a sheep in wolves clothing; it's not as big and bad as it seems. Count that "sheep" as a lesson and then take another step toward success. Falling forward is still moving forward.

I am learning to be more patient and recognize that if all I do is stand up every time I fall, I am still learning. And taking it one step at a time is enough to move forward.

Think about this—if each of us took one step each day toward a goal, then over the course of one year we would have taken 365 steps! If the average staircase is 12 stairs per staircase, that's like having risen 15 levels of staircases in one year, just by taking one step at a time! Think of it as leveling up 15 times in one year! One year, five years, 10 years will go by, whether we plan for them or not. Why wouldn't we choose progression instead of perfection? Perfection is such an elusive and unattainable goal in the world we live in. But progression? We can work with that, can't we?!

Now it's time to consider why you're here. You have your own "kiddie pool" that is making you feel in over your head. What is it in your life that you need to stand up to?

What is it in your life that you need to stand up for?

You have the power inside. You have everything you need to stand up.

The question is: will you?

As you progress through this book, your perspective will shift and you will experience a new life through a new lens. It took me many years to discover this process, and I'm challenging you to give it everything you've got, with full intention, in order to shift your perspective in 30 days.

Are you ready? Go on and take that leap of faith, you've got this!

SECTION III:
HOW TO GET THE MOST OUT OF THIS BOOK

HOW TO GET THE MOST OUT OF THIS BOOK

Here's an overview of the steps you'll implement each day.

Step 1: Change your lens.
If you were to look through a pair of eclipse glasses, the massive and brilliant sun in the sky would be reduced to a tiny dot in the distance. Sometimes we look at ourselves through a lens of doubt, fear, judgment, etc. and we feel small, less impactful, less needed, less loved. And then we live true to our fears instead of true to our dreams and goals.

To change your lens is to imagine that you're wearing a pair of dark glasses representing those negative thoughts. You look through a lens of fear and you will feel fearful. In your mind's eye, remove those imaginary dark lenses, and choose instead to look through a lens of love, hope, belief, etc.

To increase the effects of this step, imagine giving those dark lenses to your higher power. Give them away. They are not yours to keep. Next, say, "I choose to look through a lens of ____ (fill in the blank with love, belief, faith, hope, etc.) Whatever it is you need in that moment to replace the dark lens with a clear and empowering one.

There's power in making a choice. Our brains are constantly looking for evidence of whatever we believe. Making a choice bypasses the underlying negative belief, which sabotages our progress, and your brain will begin to look for evidence of the choice you made. Consider the difference in power in these statements if you don't really believe that you can. "I am capable!" (while your underlying belief is that you are weak) compared to "I choose to believe that I am capable, and to look through a lens of love for myself." Can you feel the difference?

You don't have to know exactly how to move forward, after choosing to change your lens. I encourage you to reach out to your higher power or deep into your heart and ask, "Help me understand how I can feel more capable." And your brain will go to work for you, instead of against you. Try it. It's so simple, yet life-changing.

Step 2: LISTen
Listen to what's coming to your mind and heart, write it down in a notebook, then transfer any action steps to your calendar with a date and time to complete. LIST those items on your calendar!

Listening is done by sitting in a quiet place where you feel safe and undistracted. Breath in and out deeply as you sit with a notebook and pen. My inspiration typically comes early in the morning, or late at night, but sometimes peppered between moments of the day, there are ideas I write down. Keeping a notebook with me has been a valuable way to capture those flashes of inspiration.

When ideas come to your mind and heart, it's important to write it down to show you accept and appreciate this gift. The more you take action on these, the clearer and more frequent they come in all areas of your life. Those simple and clear thoughts that come to you will be just what you need. Take a few moments each day to quiet your mind and just listen. There is plenty of research that shows benefits of resting and taking quiet time to tap into your higher power. Breathe in deeply and breathe out deeply as you listen. Trust you'll find your answers as you listen.

Some people get a flood of ideas that they jot down, while others speak their thoughts into a recorder on their phone and transcribe them later. There are many who get a flash of an idea, or a picture in their mind's eye, so they write that down. These ideas may feel exciting and joyful, but overall they are the ones that feel peaceful in your heart. Now pay attention to what happens after you capture those ideas. You'll begin to wonder, "Who am I to dream that big?" "Why would I be capable of accomplishing that goal?" That is your default programming trying to keep you safe, right in your comfort zone. But as you move through these steps, I promise you your comfort zone will expand and eventually you'll look back and wonder why you were so afraid of doing what you will be doing! Connecting to that higher power, that intuition, that flow of energy that will connect you to your innate gifts and talents that you had either forgotten, or didn't know you had. It is exhilarating! Keep at it because the mindset is like a beast that needs to be tamed. If left untamed, it will work fiercely against you.

Step 3: Take action

There is power in taking action. Sometimes we dismiss the action because we can't see how it will work out or where it will lead. Remember: action is very much like using a flashlight on a dark pathway. You can only see so far into the darkness. Once you take a step, the next step is illuminated, and the next, and so forth. You may have heard the saying that action brings clarity. It truly does. We often think our actions are taking us to a dead end. It's only when we move forward over and over again, that we find a new door leading to a pathway we never imagined. But that is only found by taking action. You don't progress unless you take a step forward.

These three steps are keys to changing perspectives and igniting your life with love and belief, which will connect you to your passions, purpose and power. Repeat them daily, along with the follow-up questions, and you will be well on your way to a new life through a new lens! And now, let's begin!

SECTION IV:
DAILY QUOTES
& WORK BOOK

DAY 1: PROGRESSION NOT PERFECTION

Perfection is impossible,
but progression?

Now that's something
I can work on.

MORNING MOMENTS

Step 1- Change your lens:

Ponder: Which negative lens is fighting for my focus?

_____

_____

(Examples: If I feel fearful or anxious about something, am I looking through a lens of doubt, fear, or judgment? Could it be a lens of criticism, fighting to be right, pride, thinking you're not good enough or loved, not talented, etc. Pay attention to how you feel and then focus on the thought that came right before that.)

Imagine: The negative thought/feeling is like a pair of dark lenses you're looking through. Say to your higher power, "Please take this lens of (fill in the blank: doubt, fear, judgment, shame, etc.), I choose instead to look through a lens of (fill in the blank: love, forgiveness, gratitude, etc.).

I choose to look through a lens of _____

Step 2—Listen:

Sit quietly and breathe deeply from your belly for a few minutes, as you allow your thoughts to flow.

> Ponder: What is tugging at my heart and mind to do, say, or learn more about today?
>
> _____
>
> _____
>
> _____
>
> _____

LIST your thoughts above, or in a separate journal, and then put any action items on your schedule or calendar, with a specific time to accomplish them.

Step 3—Take action:

Are your action items on the calendar? Now consider if you're looking through a negative lens about taking action on this. If so, repeat step 1 and change your lens again!

> Remember: Action is the most difficult, yet most transformational, part of this process. Even when you can't see how an action item will help you accomplish your goals, remember that action brings clarity, so it's time to trust the process, change your lens again if needed, and then go for it! Real progress only happens when you take action.

EVENING ACCOUNTABILITY:

What went well today?

_____

_____

What is one thing I can do to prepare for tomorrow?

_____

_____

What were the results of taking action today?

_____

_____

What follow-up item(s) became clear to me after taking action? (put them on your calendar)

_____

_____

Do I need to change my lens, as I think through any of these follow-up action items, and put any of them back on the calendar?

_____

_____

What were results of not taking action today?

_____

_____

Which lens was I looking through that prevented me from taking action?

_____

_____

Who can I share my results with and be accountable to?

_____

_____

What insight was gained by reaching out to that person for accountability?

_____

_____

If I were talking to my best friend, what would I say about the choices made if it were their day I were evaluating?

_____

_____

Two things I'm grateful for are:

_____

_____

One thing I look forward to is:

_____

DAY 2: YOU'RE NOT YOUR THOUGHTS

Thoughts define the tools you have been using; they do not define you.

If your thoughts are not serving you, then improve the tools you're working with.

MORNING MOMENTS

Step 1- Change your lens:

Ponder: Which negative lens is fighting for my focus?

_____

_____

(Examples: If I feel fearful or anxious about something, am I looking through a lens of doubt, fear, or judgment? Could it be a lens of criticism, fighting to be right, pride, thinking you're not good enough or loved, not talented, etc. Pay attention to how you feel and then focus on the thought that came right before that.)

Imagine: The negative thought/feeling is like a pair of dark lenses you're looking through. Say to your higher power, "Please take this lens of (fill in the blank: doubt, fear, judgment, shame, etc.), I choose instead to look through a lens of (fill in the blank: love, forgiveness, gratitude, etc.).

I choose to look through a lens of _____

Step 2—Listen:

Sit quietly and breathe deeply from your belly for a few minutes, as you allow your thoughts to flow.

> Ponder: What is tugging at my heart and mind to do, say, or learn more about today?
>
> _____
>
> _____
>
> _____
>
> _____

LIST your thoughts above, or in a separate journal, and then put any action items on your schedule or calendar, with a specific time to accomplish them.

Step 3—Take action:

Are your action items on the calendar? Now consider if you're looking through a negative lens about taking action on this. If so, repeat step 1 and change your lens again!

Remember: Action is the most difficult, yet most transformational, part of this process. Even when you can't see how an action item will help you accomplish your goals, remember that action brings clarity, so it's time to trust the process, change your lens again if needed, and then go for it! Real progress only happens when you take action.

EVENING ACCOUNTABILITY:

What went well today?

_____

_____

What is one thing I can do to prepare for tomorrow?

_____

_____

What were the results of taking action today?

_____

_____

What follow-up item(s) became clear to me after taking action? (put them on your calendar)

_____

_____

Do I need to change my lens, as I think through any of these follow-up action items, and put any of them back on the calendar?

_____

_____

What were results of not taking action today?

_____

_____

Which lens was I looking through that prevented me from taking action?

_____

_____

Who can I share my results with and be accountable to?

_____

_____

What insight was gained by reaching out to that person for accountability?

_____

_____

If I were talking to my best friend, what would I say about the choices made if it were their day I were evaluating?

_____

_____

Two things I'm grateful for are:

_____

_____

One thing I look forward to is:

_____

DAY 3: MINDSET IS A BEAST

Mindset is a beast. You must train the beast to

work for you or it will work fiercely against you.

MORNING MOMENTS

Step 1 - Change your lens:

Ponder: Which negative lens is fighting for my focus?

_____

_____

(Examples: If I feel fearful or anxious about something, am I looking through a lens of doubt, fear, or judgment? Could it be a lens of criticism, fighting to be right, pride, thinking you're not good enough or loved, not talented, etc. Pay attention to how you feel and then focus on the thought that came right before that.)

Imagine: The negative thought/feeling is like a pair of dark lenses you're looking through. Say to your higher power, "Please take this lens of (fill in the blank: doubt, fear, judgment, shame, etc.), I choose instead to look through a lens of (fill in the blank: love, forgiveness, gratitude, etc.).

I choose to look through a lens of _____

Step 2—Listen:

Sit quietly and breathe deeply from your belly for a few minutes, as you allow your thoughts to flow.

Ponder: What is tugging at my heart and mind to do, say, or learn more about today?

_____

_____

_____

_____

LIST your thoughts above, or in a separate journal, and then put any action items on your schedule or calendar, with a specific time to accomplish them.

Step 3—Take action:

Are your action items on the calendar? Now consider if you're looking through a negative lens about taking action on this. If so, repeat step 1 and change your lens again!

Remember: Action is the most difficult, yet most transformational, part of this process. Even when you can't see how an action item will help you accomplish your goals, remember that action brings clarity, so it's time to trust the process, change your lens again if needed, and then go for it! Real progress only happens when you take action.

EVENING ACCOUNTABILITY:

What went well today?

_____

_____

What is one thing I can do to prepare for tomorrow?

_____

_____

What were the results of taking action today?

_____

_____

What follow-up item(s) became clear to me after taking action? (put them on your calendar)

_____

_____

Do I need to change my lens, as I think through any of these follow-up action items, and put any of them back on the calendar?

_____

_____

What were results of not taking action today?

_____

_____

Which lens was I looking through that prevented me from taking action?

_____

_____

Who can I share my results with and be accountable to?

_____

_____

What insight was gained by reaching out to that person for accountability?

_____

_____

If I were talking to my best friend, what would I say about the choices made if it were their day I were evaluating?

_____

_____

Two things I'm grateful for are:

_____

_____

One thing I look forward to is:

_____

DAY 4: YOUR BRAIN TO LOOKS FOR EVIDENCE

Your brain will look for evidence of whatever you believe.

Instead of saying, "I can't," instead ask, "How can I?"

MORNING MOMENTS

Step 1 - Change your lens:

Ponder: Which negative lens is fighting for my focus?

_____

_____

(Examples: If I feel fearful or anxious about something, am I looking through a lens of doubt, fear, or judgment? Could it be a lens of criticism, fighting to be right, pride, thinking you're not good enough or loved, not talented, etc. Pay attention to how you feel and then focus on the thought that came right before that.)

Imagine: The negative thought/feeling is like a pair of dark lenses you're looking through. Say to your higher power, "Please take this lens of (fill in the blank: doubt, fear, judgment, shame, etc.), I choose instead to look through a lens of (fill in the blank: love, forgiveness, gratitude, etc.).

I choose to look through a lens of _____

Step 2—Listen:

Sit quietly and breathe deeply from your belly for a few minutes, as you allow your thoughts to flow.

Ponder: What is tugging at my heart and mind to do, say, or learn more about today?

_____

_____

_____

_____

LIST your thoughts above, or in a separate journal, and then put any action items on your schedule or calendar, with a specific time to accomplish them.

Step 3—Take action:

Are your action items on the calendar? Now consider if you're looking through a negative lens about taking action on this. If so, repeat step 1 and change your lens again!

Remember: Action is the most difficult, yet most transformational, part of this process. Even when you can't see how an action item will help you accomplish your goals, remember that action brings clarity, so it's time to trust the process, change your lens again if needed, and then go for it! Real progress only happens when you take action.

EVENING ACCOUNTABILITY:

What went well today?

_____

_____

What is one thing I can do to prepare for tomorrow?

_____

_____

What were the results of taking action today?

_____

_____

What follow-up item(s) became clear to me after taking action? (put them on your calendar)

_____

_____

Do I need to change my lens, as I think through any of these follow-up action items, and put any of them back on the calendar?

_____

_____

What were results of not taking action today?

_____

_____

Which lens was I looking through that prevented me from taking action?

_____

_____

Who can I share my results with and be accountable to?

_____

_____

What insight was gained by reaching out to that person for accountability?

_____

_____

If I were talking to my best friend, what would I say about the choices made if it were their day I were evaluating?

_____

_____

Two things I'm grateful for are:

_____

_____

One thing I look forward to is:

_____

DAY 5: POSITIVE FORCES GIVE, NEGATIVE FORCES TAKE

The more you give to positive forces, the more they give back to you.

The more you give to negative forces, the more they take from you.

MORNING MOMENTS

Step 1- Change your lens:

Ponder: Which negative lens is fighting for my focus?

_____

_____

(Examples: If I feel fearful or anxious about something, am I looking through a lens of doubt, fear, or judgment? Could it be a lens of criticism, fighting to be right, pride, thinking you're not good enough or loved, not talented, etc. Pay attention to how you feel and then focus on the thought that came right before that.)

Imagine: The negative thought/feeling is like a pair of dark lenses you're looking through. Say to your higher power, "Please take this lens of (fill in the blank: doubt, fear, judgment, shame, etc.), I choose instead to look through a lens of (fill in the blank: love, forgiveness, gratitude, etc.).

I choose to look through a lens of _____

Step 2—Listen:

Sit quietly and breathe deeply from your belly for a few minutes, as you allow your thoughts to flow.

> Ponder: What is tugging at my heart and mind to do, say, or learn more about today?
>
> _____
>
> _____
>
> _____
>
> _____

LIST your thoughts above, or in a separate journal, and then put any action items on your schedule or calendar, with a specific time to accomplish them.

Step 3—Take action:

Are your action items on the calendar? Now consider if you're looking through a negative lens about taking action on this. If so, repeat step 1 and change your lens again!

> Remember: Action is the most difficult, yet most transformational, part of this process. Even when you can't see how an action item will help you accomplish your goals, remember that action brings clarity, so it's time to trust the process, change your lens again if needed, and then go for it! Real progress only happens when you take action.

EVENING ACCOUNTABILITY:

What went well today?

_____

_____

What is one thing I can do to prepare for tomorrow?

_____

_____

What were the results of taking action today?

_____

_____

What follow-up item(s) became clear to me after taking action? (put them on your calendar)

_____

_____

Do I need to change my lens, as I think through any of these follow-up action items, and put any of them back on the calendar?

_____

_____

What were results of not taking action today?

_____

_____

Which lens was I looking through that prevented me from taking action?

_____

_____

Who can I share my results with and be accountable to?

_____

_____

What insight was gained by reaching out to that person for accountability?

_____

_____

If I were talking to my best friend, what would I say about the choices made if it were their day I were evaluating?

_____

_____

Two things I'm grateful for are:

_____

_____

One thing I look forward to is:

_____

DAY 6: THOUGHTS CREATE FEELINGS

Thoughts create feelings and feelings lead to either action or inaction.

Inaction puts you in a passive role, while focused action drives you toward your goal.

MORNING MOMENTS

Step 1- Change your lens:

Ponder: Which negative lens is fighting for my focus?

_____

_____

(Examples: If I feel fearful or anxious about something, am I looking through a lens of doubt, fear, or judgment? Could it be a lens of criticism, fighting to be right, pride, thinking you're not good enough or loved, not talented, etc. Pay attention to how you feel and then focus on the thought that came right before that.)

Imagine: The negative thought/feeling is like a pair of dark lenses you're looking through. Say to your higher power, "Please take this lens of (fill in the blank: doubt, fear, judgment, shame, etc.), I choose instead to look through a lens of (fill in the blank: love, forgiveness, gratitude, etc.).

I choose to look through a lens of _____

Step 2—Listen:

Sit quietly and breathe deeply from your belly for a few minutes, as you allow your thoughts to flow.

Ponder: What is tugging at my heart and mind to do, say, or learn more about today?

_____

_____

_____

_____

LIST your thoughts above, or in a separate journal, and then put any action items on your schedule or calendar, with a specific time to accomplish them.

Step 3—Take action:

Are your action items on the calendar? Now consider if you're looking through a negative lens about taking action on this. If so, repeat step 1 and change your lens again!

Remember: Action is the most difficult, yet most transformational, part of this process. Even when you can't see how an action item will help you accomplish your goals, remember that action brings clarity, so it's time to trust the process, change your lens again if needed, and then go for it! Real progress only happens when you take action.

EVENING ACCOUNTABILITY:

What went well today?

_____

_____

What is one thing I can do to prepare for tomorrow?

_____

_____

What were the results of taking action today?

_____

_____

What follow-up item(s) became clear to me after taking action? (put them on your calendar)

_____

_____

Do I need to change my lens, as I think through any of these follow-up action items, and put any of them back on the calendar?

_____

_____

What were results of not taking action today?

_____

_____

Which lens was I looking through that prevented me from taking action?

_____

_____

Who can I share my results with and be accountable to?

_____

_____

What insight was gained by reaching out to that person for accountability?

_____

_____

If I were talking to my best friend, what would I say about the choices made if it were their day I were evaluating?

_____

_____

Two things I'm grateful for are:

_____

_____

One thing I look forward to is:

_____

DAY 7: SIMPLE, YET ESSENTIAL

Time and again, when my world is falling apart, it's because the small and simple things have been neglected.

MORNING MOMENTS

Step 1- Change your lens:

Ponder: Which negative lens is fighting for my focus?

_____

_____

(Examples: If I feel fearful or anxious about something, am I looking through a lens of doubt, fear, or judgment? Could it be a lens of criticism, fighting to be right, pride, thinking you're not good enough or loved, not talented, etc. Pay attention to how you feel and then focus on the thought that came right before that.)

Imagine: The negative thought/feeling is like a pair of dark lenses you're looking through. Say to your higher power, "Please take this lens of (fill in the blank: doubt, fear, judgment, shame, etc.), I choose instead to look through a lens of (fill in the blank: love, forgiveness, gratitude, etc.).

I choose to look through a lens of _____

Step 2—Listen:

Sit quietly and breathe deeply from your belly for a few minutes, as you allow your thoughts to flow.

> Ponder: What is tugging at my heart and mind to do, say, or learn more about today?
>
> _____
>
> _____
>
> _____
>
> _____

LIST your thoughts above, or in a separate journal, and then put any action items on your schedule or calendar, with a specific time to accomplish them.

Step 3—Take action:

Are your action items on the calendar? Now consider if you're looking through a negative lens about taking action on this. If so, repeat step 1 and change your lens again!

> Remember: Action is the most difficult, yet most transformational, part of this process. Even when you can't see how an action item will help you accomplish your goals, remember that action brings clarity, so it's time to trust the process, change your lens again if needed, and then go for it! Real progress only happens when you take action.

EVENING ACCOUNTABILITY:

What went well today?

_____

_____

What is one thing I can do to prepare for tomorrow?

_____

_____

What were the results of taking action today?

_____

_____

What follow-up item(s) became clear to me after taking action? (put them on your calendar)

_____

_____

Do I need to change my lens, as I think through any of these follow-up action items, and put any of them back on the calendar?

_____

_____

What were results of not taking action today?

_____

_____

Which lens was I looking through that prevented me from taking action?

_____

_____

Who can I share my results with and be accountable to?

_____

_____

What insight was gained by reaching out to that person for accountability?

_____

_____

If I were talking to my best friend, what would I say about the choices made if it were their day I were evaluating?

_____

_____

Two things I'm grateful for are:

_____

_____

One thing I look forward to is:

_____

DAY 8: WEARING UNDERWEAR OVER YOUR TIGHTS

You don't have to be Superman, Elastigirl, or anyone else who wears underwear over their tights.

You are super just the way you are.

MORNING MOMENTS

Step 1- Change your lens:

Ponder: Which negative lens is fighting for my focus?

_____

_____

(Examples: If I feel fearful or anxious about something, am I looking through a lens of doubt, fear, or judgment? Could it be a lens of criticism, fighting to be right, pride, thinking you're not good enough or loved, not talented, etc. Pay attention to how you feel and then focus on the thought that came right before that.)

Imagine: The negative thought/feeling is like a pair of dark lenses you're looking through. Say to your higher power, "Please take this lens of (fill in the blank: doubt, fear, judgment, shame, etc.), I choose instead to look through a lens of (fill in the blank: love, forgiveness, gratitude, etc.).

I choose to look through a lens of _____

Step 2–Listen:

Sit quietly and breathe deeply from your belly for a few minutes, as you allow your thoughts to flow.

Ponder: What is tugging at my heart and mind to do, say, or learn more about today?

_____

_____

_____

_____

LIST your thoughts above, or in a separate journal, and then put any action items on your schedule or calendar, with a specific time to accomplish them.

Step 3–Take action:

Are your action items on the calendar? Now consider if you're looking through a negative lens about taking action on this. If so, repeat step 1 and change your lens again!

Remember: Action is the most difficult, yet most transformational, part of this process. Even when you can't see how an action item will help you accomplish your goals, remember that action brings clarity, so it's time to trust the process, change your lens again if needed, and then go for it! Real progress only happens when you take action.

EVENING ACCOUNTABILITY:

What went well today?

_____

_____

What is one thing I can do to prepare for tomorrow?

_____

_____

What were the results of taking action today?

_____

_____

What follow-up item(s) became clear to me after taking action? (put them on your calendar)

_____

_____

Do I need to change my lens, as I think through any of these follow-up action items, and put any of them back on the calendar?

_____

_____

What were results of not taking action today?

_____

_____

Which lens was I looking through that prevented me from taking action?

_____

_____

Who can I share my results with and be accountable to?

_____

_____

What insight was gained by reaching out to that person for accountability?

_____

_____

If I were talking to my best friend, what would I say about the choices made if it were their day I were evaluating?

_____

_____

Two things I'm grateful for are:

_____

_____

One thing I look forward to is:

_____

DAY 9: FAILURE IS FINITE

Failure is not forever, but will fight forever for your focus.

What you focus on is your choice.

MORNING MOMENTS

Step 1- Change your lens:

Ponder: Which negative lens is fighting for my focus?

_____

_____

(Examples: If I feel fearful or anxious about something, am I looking through a lens of doubt, fear, or judgment? Could it be a lens of criticism, fighting to be right, pride, thinking you're not good enough or loved, not talented, etc. Pay attention to how you feel and then focus on the thought that came right before that.)

Imagine: The negative thought/feeling is like a pair of dark lenses you're looking through. Say to your higher power, "Please take this lens of (fill in the blank: doubt, fear, judgment, shame, etc.), I choose instead to look through a lens of (fill in the blank: love, forgiveness, gratitude, etc.).

I choose to look through a lens of _____

Step 2—Listen:

Sit quietly and breathe deeply from your belly for a few minutes, as you allow your thoughts to flow.

> Ponder: What is tugging at my heart and mind to do, say, or learn more about today?
>
> _____
>
> _____
>
> _____
>
> _____

LIST your thoughts above, or in a separate journal, and then put any action items on your schedule or calendar, with a specific time to accomplish them.

Step 3—Take action:

Are your action items on the calendar? Now consider if you're looking through a negative lens about taking action on this. If so, repeat step 1 and change your lens again!

> Remember: Action is the most difficult, yet most transformational, part of this process. Even when you can't see how an action item will help you accomplish your goals, remember that action brings clarity, so it's time to trust the process, change your lens again if needed, and then go for it! Real progress only happens when you take action.

EVENING ACCOUNTABILITY:

What went well today?

_____

_____

What is one thing I can do to prepare for tomorrow?

_____

_____

What were the results of taking action today?

_____

_____

What follow-up item(s) became clear to me after taking action? (put them on your calendar)

_____

_____

Do I need to change my lens, as I think through any of these follow-up action items, and put any of them back on the calendar?

_____

_____

What were results of not taking action today?

_____

_____

Which lens was I looking through that prevented me from taking action?

_____

_____

Who can I share my results with and be accountable to?

_____

_____

What insight was gained by reaching out to that person for accountability?

_____

_____

If I were talking to my best friend, what would I say about the choices made if it were their day I were evaluating?

_____

_____

Two things I'm grateful for are:

_____

_____

One thing I look forward to is:

_____

DAY 10: YOU ARE THE ONLY ONE

You're the only one responsible for

believing in yourself and for taking action.

MORNING MOMENTS

Step 1- Change your lens:

Ponder: Which negative lens is fighting for my focus?

_____

_____

(Examples: If I feel fearful or anxious about something, am I looking through a lens of doubt, fear, or judgment? Could it be a lens of criticism, fighting to be right, pride, thinking you're not good enough or loved, not talented, etc. Pay attention to how you feel and then focus on the thought that came right before that.)

Imagine: The negative thought/feeling is like a pair of dark lenses you're looking through. Say to your higher power, "Please take this lens of (fill in the blank: doubt, fear, judgment, shame, etc.), I choose instead to look through a lens of (fill in the blank: love, forgiveness, gratitude, etc.).

I choose to look through a lens of _____

Step 2—Listen:

Sit quietly and breathe deeply from your belly for a few minutes, as you allow your thoughts to flow.

Ponder: What is tugging at my heart and mind to do, say, or learn more about today?

_____

_____

_____

_____

LIST your thoughts above, or in a separate journal, and then put any action items on your schedule or calendar, with a specific time to accomplish them.

Step 3—Take action:

Are your action items on the calendar? Now consider if you're looking through a negative lens about taking action on this. If so, repeat step 1 and change your lens again!

Remember: Action is the most difficult, yet most transformational, part of this process. Even when you can't see how an action item will help you accomplish your goals, remember that action brings clarity, so it's time to trust the process, change your lens again if needed, and then go for it! Real progress only happens when you take action.

EVENING ACCOUNTABILITY:

What went well today?

_____

_____

What is one thing I can do to prepare for tomorrow?

_____

_____

What were the results of taking action today?

_____

_____

What follow-up item(s) became clear to me after taking action? (put them on your calendar)

_____

_____

Do I need to change my lens, as I think through any of these follow-up action items, and put any of them back on the calendar?

_____

_____

What were results of not taking action today?

_____

_____

Which lens was I looking through that prevented me from taking action?

_____

_____

Who can I share my results with and be accountable to?

_____

_____

What insight was gained by reaching out to that person for accountability?

_____

_____

If I were talking to my best friend, what would I say about the choices made if it were their day I were evaluating?

_____

_____

Two things I'm grateful for are:

_____

_____

One thing I look forward to is:

_____

DAY 11: GROWING PAINS

Growing pains that come from making mistakes are part of the process and markers of progress.

MORNING MOMENTS

Step 1- Change your lens:

Ponder: Which negative lens is fighting for my focus?

_____

_____

(Examples: If I feel fearful or anxious about something, am I looking through a lens of doubt, fear, or judgment? Could it be a lens of criticism, fighting to be right, pride, thinking you're not good enough or loved, not talented, etc. Pay attention to how you feel and then focus on the thought that came right before that.)

Imagine: The negative thought/feeling is like a pair of dark lenses you're looking through. Say to your higher power, "Please take this lens of (fill in the blank: doubt, fear, judgment, shame, etc.), I choose instead to look through a lens of (fill in the blank: love, forgiveness, gratitude, etc.).

I choose to look through a lens of _____

Step 2—Listen:

Sit quietly and breathe deeply from your belly for a few minutes, as you allow your thoughts to flow.

Ponder: What is tugging at my heart and mind to do, say, or learn more about today?

_____

_____

_____

_____

LIST your thoughts above, or in a separate journal, and then put any action items on your schedule or calendar, with a specific time to accomplish them.

Step 3—Take action:

Are your action items on the calendar? Now consider if you're looking through a negative lens about taking action on this. If so, repeat step 1 and change your lens again!

Remember: Action is the most difficult, yet most transformational, part of this process. Even when you can't see how an action item will help you accomplish your goals, remember that action brings clarity, so it's time to trust the process, change your lens again if needed, and then go for it! Real progress only happens when you take action.

EVENING ACCOUNTABILITY:

What went well today?

_____

_____

What is one thing I can do to prepare for tomorrow?

_____

_____

What were the results of taking action today?

_____

_____

What follow-up item(s) became clear to me after taking action? (put them on your calendar)

_____

_____

Do I need to change my lens, as I think through any of these follow-up action items, and put any of them back on the calendar?

_____

_____

What were results of not taking action today?

_____

_____

Which lens was I looking through that prevented me from taking action?

_____

_____

Who can I share my results with and be accountable to?

_____

_____

What insight was gained by reaching out to that person for accountability?

_____

_____

If I were talking to my best friend, what would I say about the choices made if it were their day I were evaluating?

_____

_____

Two things I'm grateful for are:

_____

_____

One thing I look forward to is:

_____

DAY 12: FAILURE IS AN ILLUSION

I don't believe in failure because there's always a lesson to be learned and a task that can be done.

MORNING MOMENTS

Step 1- Change your lens:

Ponder: Which negative lens is fighting for my focus?

_____

_____

(Examples: If I feel fearful or anxious about something, am I looking through a lens of doubt, fear, or judgment? Could it be a lens of criticism, fighting to be right, pride, thinking you're not good enough or loved, not talented, etc. Pay attention to how you feel and then focus on the thought that came right before that.)

Imagine: The negative thought/feeling is like a pair of dark lenses you're looking through. Say to your higher power, "Please take this lens of (fill in the blank: doubt, fear, judgment, shame, etc.), I choose instead to look through a lens of (fill in the blank: love, forgiveness, gratitude, etc.).

I choose to look through a lens of _____

Step 2—Listen:

Sit quietly and breathe deeply from your belly for a few minutes, as you allow your thoughts to flow.

> Ponder: What is tugging at my heart and mind to do, say, or learn more about today?
>
> _____
>
> _____
>
> _____
>
> _____

LIST your thoughts above, or in a separate journal, and then put any action items on your schedule or calendar, with a specific time to accomplish them.

Step 3—Take action:

Are your action items on the calendar? Now consider if you're looking through a negative lens about taking action on this. If so, repeat step 1 and change your lens again!

> Remember: Action is the most difficult, yet most transformational, part of this process. Even when you can't see how an action item will help you accomplish your goals, remember that action brings clarity, so it's time to trust the process, change your lens again if needed, and then go for it! Real progress only happens when you take action.

EVENING ACCOUNTABILITY:

What went well today?

_____

_____

What is one thing I can do to prepare for tomorrow?

_____

_____

What were the results of taking action today?

_____

_____

What follow-up item(s) became clear to me after taking action? (put them on your calendar)

_____

_____

Do I need to change my lens, as I think through any of these follow-up action items, and put any of them back on the calendar?

_____

_____

What were results of not taking action today?

_____

_____

Which lens was I looking through that prevented me from taking action?

_____

_____

Who can I share my results with and be accountable to?

_____

_____

What insight was gained by reaching out to that person for accountability?

_____

_____

If I were talking to my best friend, what would I say about the choices made if it were their day I were evaluating?

_____

_____

Two things I'm grateful for are:

_____

_____

One thing I look forward to is:

_____

DAY 13: WHEN DREAMS TUG AT YOUR HEART

When those dreams tug at your heart and mind, instead of fearfully asking, "Why would I?"

Confidently shout out, "Why wouldn't I!"

MORNING MOMENTS

Step 1- Change your lens:

Ponder: Which negative lens is fighting for my focus?

_____

_____

(Examples: If I feel fearful or anxious about something, am I looking through a lens of doubt, fear, or judgment? Could it be a lens of criticism, fighting to be right, pride, thinking you're not good enough or loved, not talented, etc. Pay attention to how you feel and then focus on the thought that came right before that.)

Imagine: The negative thought/feeling is like a pair of dark lenses you're looking through. Say to your higher power, "Please take this lens of (fill in the blank: doubt, fear, judgment, shame, etc.), I choose instead to look through a lens of (fill in the blank: love, forgiveness, gratitude, etc.).

I choose to look through a lens of _____

Step 2—Listen:
Sit quietly and breathe deeply from your belly for a few minutes, as you allow your thoughts to flow.

> Ponder: What is tugging at my heart and mind to do, say, or learn more about today?
>
> _____
>
> _____
>
> _____
>
> _____

LIST your thoughts above, or in a separate journal, and then put any action items on your schedule or calendar, with a specific time to accomplish them.

Step 3—Take action:
Are your action items on the calendar? Now consider if you're looking through a negative lens about taking action on this. If so, repeat step 1 and change your lens again!

> Remember: Action is the most difficult, yet most transformational, part of this process. Even when you can't see how an action item will help you accomplish your goals, remember that action brings clarity, so it's time to trust the process, change your lens again if needed, and then go for it! Real progress only happens when you take action.

EVENING ACCOUNTABILITY:

What went well today?

_____

_____

What is one thing I can do to prepare for tomorrow?

_____

_____

What were the results of taking action today?

_____

_____

What follow-up item(s) became clear to me after taking action? (put them on your calendar)

_____

_____

Do I need to change my lens, as I think through any of these follow-up action items, and put any of them back on the calendar?

_____

_____

What were results of not taking action today?

_____

_____

Which lens was I looking through that prevented me from taking action?

_____

_____

Who can I share my results with and be accountable to?

_____

_____

What insight was gained by reaching out to that person for accountability?

_____

_____

If I were talking to my best friend, what would I say about the choices made if it were their day I were evaluating?

_____

_____

Two things I'm grateful for are:

_____

_____

One thing I look forward to is:

_____

DAY 14: FAILURE IS A LESSON

Failure is merely a sheep in wolf's clothing; it's not as big or bad as it seems.

Count failure as another lesson on the pathway toward success.

MORNING MOMENTS

Step 1- Change your lens:

Ponder: Which negative lens is fighting for my focus?

_____

_____

(Examples: If I feel fearful or anxious about something, am I looking through a lens of doubt, fear, or judgment? Could it be a lens of criticism, fighting to be right, pride, thinking you're not good enough or loved, not talented, etc. Pay attention to how you feel and then focus on the thought that came right before that.)

Imagine: The negative thought/feeling is like a pair of dark lenses you're looking through. Say to your higher power, "Please take this lens of (fill in the blank: doubt, fear, judgment, shame, etc.), I choose instead to look through a lens of (fill in the blank: love, forgiveness, gratitude, etc.).

I choose to look through a lens of _____

Step 2—Listen:

Sit quietly and breathe deeply from your belly for a few minutes, as you allow your thoughts to flow.

Ponder: What is tugging at my heart and mind to do, say, or learn more about today?

_____

_____

_____

_____

LIST your thoughts above, or in a separate journal, and then put any action items on your schedule or calendar, with a specific time to accomplish them.

Step 3—Take action:

Are your action items on the calendar? Now consider if you're looking through a negative lens about taking action on this. If so, repeat step 1 and change your lens again!

Remember: Action is the most difficult, yet most transformational, part of this process. Even when you can't see how an action item will help you accomplish your goals, remember that action brings clarity, so it's time to trust the process, change your lens again if needed, and then go for it! Real progress only happens when you take action.

EVENING ACCOUNTABILITY:

What went well today?

_____

_____

What is one thing I can do to prepare for tomorrow?

_____

_____

What were the results of taking action today?

_____

_____

What follow-up item(s) became clear to me after taking action? (put them on your calendar)

_____

_____

Do I need to change my lens, as I think through any of these follow-up action items, and put any of them back on the calendar?

_____

_____

What were results of not taking action today?

_____

_____

Which lens was I looking through that prevented me from taking action?

_____

_____

Who can I share my results with and be accountable to?

_____

_____

What insight was gained by reaching out to that person for accountability?

_____

_____

If I were talking to my best friend, what would I say about the choices made if it were their day I were evaluating?

_____

_____

Two things I'm grateful for are:

_____

_____

One thing I look forward to is:

_____

DAY 15: LISTEN TO THE NUDGES

Listen to those little nudges that pull at your heart and mind; they will never steer you wrong.

MORNING MOMENTS

Step 1- Change your lens:

Ponder: Which negative lens is fighting for my focus?

_____

_____

(Examples: If I feel fearful or anxious about something, am I looking through a lens of doubt, fear, or judgment? Could it be a lens of criticism, fighting to be right, pride, thinking you're not good enough or loved, not talented, etc. Pay attention to how you feel and then focus on the thought that came right before that.)

Imagine: The negative thought/feeling is like a pair of dark lenses you're looking through. Say to your higher power, "Please take this lens of (fill in the blank: doubt, fear, judgment, shame, etc.), I choose instead to look through a lens of (fill in the blank: love, forgiveness, gratitude, etc.).

I choose to look through a lens of _____

Step 2—Listen:

Sit quietly and breathe deeply from your belly for a few minutes, as you allow your thoughts to flow.

Ponder: What is tugging at my heart and mind to do, say, or learn more about today?

_____

_____

_____

_____

LIST your thoughts above, or in a separate journal, and then put any action items on your schedule or calendar, with a specific time to accomplish them.

Step 3—Take action:

Are your action items on the calendar? Now consider if you're looking through a negative lens about taking action on this. If so, repeat step 1 and change your lens again!

Remember: Action is the most difficult, yet most transformational, part of this process. Even when you can't see how an action item will help you accomplish your goals, remember that action brings clarity, so it's time to trust the process, change your lens again if needed, and then go for it! Real progress only happens when you take action.

EVENING ACCOUNTABILITY:

What went well today?

_____

_____

What is one thing I can do to prepare for tomorrow?

_____

_____

What were the results of taking action today?

_____

_____

What follow-up item(s) became clear to me after taking action? (put them on your calendar)

_____

_____

Do I need to change my lens, as I think through any of these follow-up action items, and put any of them back on the calendar?

_____

_____

What were results of not taking action today?

_____

_____

Which lens was I looking through that prevented me from taking action?

_____

_____

Who can I share my results with and be accountable to?

_____

_____

What insight was gained by reaching out to that person for accountability?

_____

_____

If I were talking to my best friend, what would I say about the choices made if it were their day I were evaluating?

_____

_____

Two things I'm grateful for are:

_____

_____

One thing I look forward to is:

_____

DAY 16: DON'T WAIT UNTIL YOU FEEL LIKE IT

Waiting until you feel like it
cheats you out of finishing.

Only finishers accomplish
their goals.

MORNING MOMENTS

Step 1- Change your lens:

Ponder: Which negative lens is fighting for my focus?

_____

_____

(Examples: If I feel fearful or anxious about something, am I looking through a lens of doubt, fear, or judgment? Could it be a lens of criticism, fighting to be right, pride, thinking you're not good enough or loved, not talented, etc. Pay attention to how you feel and then focus on the thought that came right before that.)

Imagine: The negative thought/feeling is like a pair of dark lenses you're looking through. Say to your higher power, "Please take this lens of (fill in the blank: doubt, fear, judgment, shame, etc.), I choose instead to look through a lens of (fill in the blank: love, forgiveness, gratitude, etc.).

I choose to look through a lens of _____

Step 2—Listen:

Sit quietly and breathe deeply from your belly for a few minutes, as you allow your thoughts to flow.

Ponder: What is tugging at my heart and mind to do, say, or learn more about today?

_____

_____

_____

_____

LIST your thoughts above, or in a separate journal, and then put any action items on your schedule or calendar, with a specific time to accomplish them.

Step 3—Take action:

Are your action items on the calendar? Now consider if you're looking through a negative lens about taking action on this. If so, repeat step 1 and change your lens again!

Remember: Action is the most difficult, yet most transformational, part of this process. Even when you can't see how an action item will help you accomplish your goals, remember that action brings clarity, so it's time to trust the process, change your lens again if needed, and then go for it! Real progress only happens when you take action.

EVENING ACCOUNTABILITY:

What went well today?

_____

_____

What is one thing I can do to prepare for tomorrow?

_____

_____

What were the results of taking action today?

_____

_____

What follow-up item(s) became clear to me after taking action? (put them on your calendar)

_____

_____

Do I need to change my lens, as I think through any of these follow-up action items, and put any of them back on the calendar?

_____

_____

What were results of not taking action today?

_____

_____

Which lens was I looking through that prevented me from taking action?

_____

_____

Who can I share my results with and be accountable to?

_____

_____

What insight was gained by reaching out to that person for accountability?

_____

_____

If I were talking to my best friend, what would I say about the choices made if it were their day I were evaluating?

_____

_____

Two things I'm grateful for are:

_____

_____

One thing I look forward to is:

_____

DAY 17: KNOW WHAT YOU STAND FOR

It's just as important to know what you will stand for as it is to know what you will not stand for.

MORNING MOMENTS

Step 1- Change your lens:

Ponder: Which negative lens is fighting for my focus?

_____

_____

(Examples: If I feel fearful or anxious about something, am I looking through a lens of doubt, fear, or judgment? Could it be a lens of criticism, fighting to be right, pride, thinking you're not good enough or loved, not talented, etc. Pay attention to how you feel and then focus on the thought that came right before that.)

Imagine: The negative thought/feeling is like a pair of dark lenses you're looking through. Say to your higher power, "Please take this lens of (fill in the blank: doubt, fear, judgment, shame, etc.), I choose instead to look through a lens of (fill in the blank: love, forgiveness, gratitude, etc.).

I choose to look through a lens of _____

Step 2—Listen:

Sit quietly and breathe deeply from your belly for a few minutes, as you allow your thoughts to flow.

Ponder: What is tugging at my heart and mind to do, say, or learn more about today?

_____

_____

_____

_____

LIST your thoughts above, or in a separate journal, and then put any action items on your schedule or calendar, with a specific time to accomplish them.

Step 3—Take action:

Are your action items on the calendar? Now consider if you're looking through a negative lens about taking action on this. If so, repeat step 1 and change your lens again!

Remember: Action is the most difficult, yet most transformational, part of this process. Even when you can't see how an action item will help you accomplish your goals, remember that action brings clarity, so it's time to trust the process, change your lens again if needed, and then go for it! Real progress only happens when you take action.

EVENING ACCOUNTABILITY:

What went well today?

_____

_____

What is one thing I can do to prepare for tomorrow?

_____

_____

What were the results of taking action today?

_____

_____

What follow-up item(s) became clear to me after taking action? (put them on your calendar)

_____

_____

Do I need to change my lens, as I think through any of these follow-up action items, and put any of them back on the calendar?

_____

_____

What were results of not taking action today?

_____

_____

Which lens was I looking through that prevented me from taking action?

_____

_____

Who can I share my results with and be accountable to?

_____

_____

What insight was gained by reaching out to that person for accountability?

_____

_____

If I were talking to my best friend, what would I say about the choices made if it were their day I were evaluating?

_____

_____

Two things I'm grateful for are:

_____

_____

One thing I look forward to is:

_____

DAY 18: DON'T DISCOUNT THE SMALL STEPS

Don't discount the small steps. Over time, they are the big steps.

MORNING MOMENTS

Step 1- Change your lens:

Ponder: Which negative lens is fighting for my focus?

_____

_____

(Examples: If I feel fearful or anxious about something, am I looking through a lens of doubt, fear, or judgment? Could it be a lens of criticism, fighting to be right, pride, thinking you're not good enough or loved, not talented, etc. Pay attention to how you feel and then focus on the thought that came right before that.)

Imagine: The negative thought/feeling is like a pair of dark lenses you're looking through. Say to your higher power, "Please take this lens of (fill in the blank: doubt, fear, judgment, shame, etc.), I choose instead to look through a lens of (fill in the blank: love, forgiveness, gratitude, etc.).

I choose to look through a lens of _____

Step 2–Listen:

Sit quietly and breathe deeply from your belly for a few minutes, as you allow your thoughts to flow.

> Ponder: What is tugging at my heart and mind to do, say, or learn more about today?
>
> _____
>
> _____
>
> _____
>
> _____

LIST your thoughts above, or in a separate journal, and then put any action items on your schedule or calendar, with a specific time to accomplish them.

Step 3–Take action:

Are your action items on the calendar? Now consider if you're looking through a negative lens about taking action on this. If so, repeat step 1 and change your lens again!

> Remember: Action is the most difficult, yet most transformational, part of this process. Even when you can't see how an action item will help you accomplish your goals, remember that action brings clarity, so it's time to trust the process, change your lens again if needed, and then go for it! Real progress only happens when you take action.

EVENING ACCOUNTABILITY:

What went well today?

_____

_____

What is one thing I can do to prepare for tomorrow?

_____

_____

What were the results of taking action today?

_____

_____

What follow-up item(s) became clear to me after taking action? (put them on your calendar)

_____

_____

Do I need to change my lens, as I think through any of these follow-up action items, and put any of them back on the calendar?

_____

_____

What were results of not taking action today?

_____

_____

Which lens was I looking through that prevented me from taking action?

_____

_____

Who can I share my results with and be accountable to?

_____

_____

What insight was gained by reaching out to that person for accountability?

_____

_____

If I were talking to my best friend, what would I say about the choices made if it were their day I were evaluating?

_____

_____

Two things I'm grateful for are:

_____

_____

One thing I look forward to is:

_____

DAY 19: WE'RE ALL HYPOCRITES ANYWAY

It is human to be a hypocrite, yet we're often too quick to point out others hypocrisy. Remember that the only one we can change is ourselves.

Stop judging. Start loving. Keep trying.

MORNING MOMENTS

Step 1 - Change your lens:

Ponder: Which negative lens is fighting for my focus?

_____

_____

(Examples: If I feel fearful or anxious about something, am I looking through a lens of doubt, fear, or judgment? Could it be a lens of criticism, fighting to be right, pride, thinking you're not good enough or loved, not talented, etc. Pay attention to how you feel and then focus on the thought that came right before that.)

Imagine: The negative thought/feeling is like a pair of dark lenses you're looking through. Say to your higher power, "Please take this lens of (fill in the blank: doubt, fear, judgment, shame, etc.), I choose instead to look through a lens of (fill in the blank: love, forgiveness, gratitude, etc.).

I choose to look through a lens of _____

Step 2–Listen:

Sit quietly and breathe deeply from your belly for a few minutes, as you allow your thoughts to flow.

Ponder: What is tugging at my heart and mind to do, say, or learn more about today?

_____

_____

_____

_____

LIST your thoughts above, or in a separate journal, and then put any action items on your schedule or calendar, with a specific time to accomplish them.

Step 3–Take action:

Are your action items on the calendar? Now consider if you're looking through a negative lens about taking action on this. If so, repeat step 1 and change your lens again!

Remember: Action is the most difficult, yet most transformational, part of this process. Even when you can't see how an action item will help you accomplish your goals, remember that action brings clarity, so it's time to trust the process, change your lens again if needed, and then go for it! Real progress only happens when you take action.

EVENING ACCOUNTABILITY:

What went well today?

_____

_____

What is one thing I can do to prepare for tomorrow?

_____

_____

What were the results of taking action today?

_____

_____

What follow-up item(s) became clear to me after taking action? (put them on your calendar)

_____

_____

Do I need to change my lens, as I think through any of these follow-up action items, and put any of them back on the calendar?

_____

_____

What were results of not taking action today?

_____

_____

Which lens was I looking through that prevented me from taking action?

_____

_____

Who can I share my results with and be accountable to?

_____

_____

What insight was gained by reaching out to that person for accountability?

_____

_____

If I were talking to my best friend, what would I say about the choices made if it were their day I were evaluating?

_____

_____

Two things I'm grateful for are:

_____

_____

One thing I look forward to is:

_____

DAY 20: PAYING FOR PROCRASTINATION

Procrastinate now and
pay for it later.

Be proactive now and reap
the rewards now and later.

MORNING MOMENTS

Step 1- Change your lens:

Ponder: Which negative lens is fighting for my focus?

_____

_____

(Examples: If I feel fearful or anxious about something, am I looking through a lens of doubt, fear, or judgment? Could it be a lens of criticism, fighting to be right, pride, thinking you're not good enough or loved, not talented, etc. Pay attention to how you feel and then focus on the thought that came right before that.)

Imagine: The negative thought/feeling is like a pair of dark lenses you're looking through. Say to your higher power, "Please take this lens of (fill in the blank: doubt, fear, judgment, shame, etc.), I choose instead to look through a lens of (fill in the blank: love, forgiveness, gratitude, etc.).

I choose to look through a lens of _____

Step 2—Listen:

Sit quietly and breathe deeply from your belly for a few minutes, as you allow your thoughts to flow.

Ponder: What is tugging at my heart and mind to do, say, or learn more about today?

_____

_____

_____

_____

LIST your thoughts above, or in a separate journal, and then put any action items on your schedule or calendar, with a specific time to accomplish them.

Step 3—Take action:

Are your action items on the calendar? Now consider if you're looking through a negative lens about taking action on this. If so, repeat step 1 and change your lens again!

Remember: Action is the most difficult, yet most transformational, part of this process. Even when you can't see how an action item will help you accomplish your goals, remember that action brings clarity, so it's time to trust the process, change your lens again if needed, and then go for it! Real progress only happens when you take action.

EVENING ACCOUNTABILITY:

What went well today?

_____

_____

What is one thing I can do to prepare for tomorrow?

_____

_____

What were the results of taking action today?

_____

_____

What follow-up item(s) became clear to me after taking action? (put them on your calendar)

_____

_____

Do I need to change my lens, as I think through any of these follow-up action items, and put any of them back on the calendar?

_____

_____

What were results of not taking action today?

_____

_____

Which lens was I looking through that prevented me from taking action?

_____

_____

Who can I share my results with and be accountable to?

_____

_____

What insight was gained by reaching out to that person for accountability?

_____

_____

If I were talking to my best friend, what would I say about the choices made if it were their day I were evaluating?

_____

_____

Two things I'm grateful for are:

_____

_____

One thing I look forward to is:

_____

DAY 21: TRUE FAILURE IS QUITTING

Failure lies not in falling flat on our faces, but in failing to focus on the lesson, and try again.

MORNING MOMENTS

Step 1- Change your lens:

Ponder: Which negative lens is fighting for my focus?

_____

_____

(Examples: If I feel fearful or anxious about something, am I looking through a lens of doubt, fear, or judgment? Could it be a lens of criticism, fighting to be right, pride, thinking you're not good enough or loved, not talented, etc. Pay attention to how you feel and then focus on the thought that came right before that.)

Imagine: The negative thought/feeling is like a pair of dark lenses you're looking through. Say to your higher power, "Please take this lens of (fill in the blank: doubt, fear, judgment, shame, etc.), I choose instead to look through a lens of (fill in the blank: love, forgiveness, gratitude, etc.).

I choose to look through a lens of _____

Step 2—Listen:

Sit quietly and breathe deeply from your belly for a few minutes, as you allow your thoughts to flow.

> Ponder: What is tugging at my heart and mind to do, say, or learn more about today?
>
> _____
>
> _____
>
> _____
>
> _____

LIST your thoughts above, or in a separate journal, and then put any action items on your schedule or calendar, with a specific time to accomplish them.

Step 3—Take action:

Are your action items on the calendar? Now consider if you're looking through a negative lens about taking action on this. If so, repeat step 1 and change your lens again!

> Remember: Action is the most difficult, yet most transformational, part of this process. Even when you can't see how an action item will help you accomplish your goals, remember that action brings clarity, so it's time to trust the process, change your lens again if needed, and then go for it! Real progress only happens when you take action.

EVENING ACCOUNTABILITY:

What went well today?

_____

_____

What is one thing I can do to prepare for tomorrow?

_____

_____

What were the results of taking action today?

_____

_____

What follow-up item(s) became clear to me after taking action? (put them on your calendar)

_____

_____

Do I need to change my lens, as I think through any of these follow-up action items, and put any of them back on the calendar?

_____

_____

What were results of not taking action today?

_____

_____

Which lens was I looking through that prevented me from taking action?

_____

_____

Who can I share my results with and be accountable to?

_____

_____

What insight was gained by reaching out to that person for accountability?

_____

_____

If I were talking to my best friend, what would I say about the choices made if it were their day I were evaluating?

_____

_____

Two things I'm grateful for are:

_____

_____

One thing I look forward to is:

_____

DAY 22: DON'T PROVE, JUST IMPROVE

It's not so much about proving myself to others as it is about improving myself for others.

MORNING MOMENTS

Step 1- Change your lens:

Ponder: Which negative lens is fighting for my focus?

_____

_____

(Examples: If I feel fearful or anxious about something, am I looking through a lens of doubt, fear, or judgment? Could it be a lens of criticism, fighting to be right, pride, thinking you're not good enough or loved, not talented, etc. Pay attention to how you feel and then focus on the thought that came right before that.)

Imagine: The negative thought/feeling is like a pair of dark lenses you're looking through. Say to your higher power, "Please take this lens of (fill in the blank: doubt, fear, judgment, shame, etc.), I choose instead to look through a lens of (fill in the blank: love, forgiveness, gratitude, etc.).

I choose to look through a lens of _____

Step 2—Listen:

Sit quietly and breathe deeply from your belly for a few minutes, as you allow your thoughts to flow.

Ponder: What is tugging at my heart and mind to do, say, or learn more about today?

_____

_____

_____

_____

LIST your thoughts above, or in a separate journal, and then put any action items on your schedule or calendar, with a specific time to accomplish them.

Step 3—Take action:

Are your action items on the calendar? Now consider if you're looking through a negative lens about taking action on this. If so, repeat step 1 and change your lens again!

Remember: Action is the most difficult, yet most transformational, part of this process. Even when you can't see how an action item will help you accomplish your goals, remember that action brings clarity, so it's time to trust the process, change your lens again if needed, and then go for it! Real progress only happens when you take action.

EVENING ACCOUNTABILITY:

What went well today?

_____

_____

What is one thing I can do to prepare for tomorrow?

_____

_____

What were the results of taking action today?

_____

_____

What follow-up item(s) became clear to me after taking action? (put them on your calendar)

_____

_____

Do I need to change my lens, as I think through any of these follow-up action items, and put any of them back on the calendar?

_____

_____

What were results of not taking action today?

_____

_____

Which lens was I looking through that prevented me from taking action?

_____

_____

Who can I share my results with and be accountable to?

_____

_____

What insight was gained by reaching out to that person for accountability?

_____

_____

If I were talking to my best friend, what would I say about the choices made if it were their day I were evaluating?

_____

_____

Two things I'm grateful for are:

_____

_____

One thing I look forward to is:

_____

DAY 23: ASK EMPOWERING QUESTIONS

Instead of asking, "What will go wrong?" Ask empowering questions such as, "What if it turns out better than imagined? What if I do succeed? What if I love this?"

MORNING MOMENTS

Step 1- Change your lens:

Ponder: Which negative lens is fighting for my focus?

_____

_____

(Examples: If I feel fearful or anxious about something, am I looking through a lens of doubt, fear, or judgment? Could it be a lens of criticism, fighting to be right, pride, thinking you're not good enough or loved, not talented, etc. Pay attention to how you feel and then focus on the thought that came right before that.)

Imagine: The negative thought/feeling is like a pair of dark lenses you're looking through. Say to your higher power, "Please take this lens of (fill in the blank: doubt, fear, judgment, shame, etc.), I choose instead to look through a lens of (fill in the blank: love, forgiveness, gratitude, etc.).

I choose to look through a lens of _____

Step 2—Listen:
Sit quietly and breathe deeply from your belly for a few minutes, as you allow your thoughts to flow.

> Ponder: What is tugging at my heart and mind to do, say, or learn more about today?
>
> _____
>
> _____
>
> _____
>
> _____

LIST your thoughts above, or in a separate journal, and then put any action items on your schedule or calendar, with a specific time to accomplish them.

Step 3—Take action:
Are your action items on the calendar? Now consider if you're looking through a negative lens about taking action on this. If so, repeat step 1 and change your lens again!

> Remember: Action is the most difficult, yet most transformational, part of this process. Even when you can't see how an action item will help you accomplish your goals, remember that action brings clarity, so it's time to trust the process, change your lens again if needed, and then go for it! Real progress only happens when you take action.

EVENING ACCOUNTABILITY:

What went well today?

_____

_____

What is one thing I can do to prepare for tomorrow?

_____

_____

What were the results of taking action today?

_____

_____

What follow-up item(s) became clear to me after taking action? (put them on your calendar)

_____

_____

Do I need to change my lens, as I think through any of these follow-up action items, and put any of them back on the calendar?

_____

_____

What were results of not taking action today?

_____

_____

Which lens was I looking through that prevented me from taking action?

_____

_____

Who can I share my results with and be accountable to?

_____

_____

What insight was gained by reaching out to that person for accountability?

_____

_____

If I were talking to my best friend, what would I say about the choices made if it were their day I were evaluating?

_____

_____

Two things I'm grateful for are:

_____

_____

One thing I look forward to is:

_____

DAY 24: GAIN CONFIDENCE & CLARITY

Confidence & Clarity
don't come BEFORE you
take action. They come
BECAUSE you take action.

MORNING MOMENTS

Step 1- Change your lens:

Ponder: Which negative lens is fighting for my focus?

_____

_____

(Examples: If I feel fearful or anxious about something, am I looking through a lens of doubt, fear, or judgment? Could it be a lens of criticism, fighting to be right, pride, thinking you're not good enough or loved, not talented, etc. Pay attention to how you feel and then focus on the thought that came right before that.)

Imagine: The negative thought/feeling is like a pair of dark lenses you're looking through. Say to your higher power, "Please take this lens of (fill in the blank: doubt, fear, judgment, shame, etc.), I choose instead to look through a lens of (fill in the blank: love, forgiveness, gratitude, etc.).

I choose to look through a lens of _____

Step 2-Listen:

Sit quietly and breathe deeply from your belly for a few minutes, as you allow your thoughts to flow.

> Ponder: What is tugging at my heart and mind to do, say, or learn more about today?
>
> _____
>
> _____
>
> _____
>
> _____

LIST your thoughts above, or in a separate journal, and then put any action items on your schedule or calendar, with a specific time to accomplish them.

Step 3-Take action:

Are your action items on the calendar? Now consider if you're looking through a negative lens about taking action on this. If so, repeat step 1 and change your lens again!

> Remember: Action is the most difficult, yet most transformational, part of this process. Even when you can't see how an action item will help you accomplish your goals, remember that action brings clarity, so it's time to trust the process, change your lens again if needed, and then go for it! Real progress only happens when you take action.

EVENING ACCOUNTABILITY:

What went well today?

_____

_____

What is one thing I can do to prepare for tomorrow?

_____

_____

What were the results of taking action today?

_____

_____

What follow-up item(s) became clear to me after
taking action? (put them on your calendar)

_____

_____

Do I need to change my lens, as I think through any of
these follow-up action items, and put any of them back
on the calendar?

_____

_____

What were results of not taking action today?

_____

_____

Which lens was I looking through that prevented me from taking action?

_____

_____

Who can I share my results with and be accountable to?

_____

_____

What insight was gained by reaching out to that person for accountability?

_____

_____

If I were talking to my best friend, what would I say about the choices made if it were their day I were evaluating?

_____

_____

Two things I'm grateful for are:

_____

_____

One thing I look forward to is:

_____

DAY 25: PLAN WITH PURPOSE

Plan with purpose, pay the price, reap the reward.

MORNING MOMENTS

Step 1- Change your lens:

Ponder: Which negative lens is fighting for my focus?

_____

_____

(Examples: If I feel fearful or anxious about something, am I looking through a lens of doubt, fear, or judgment? Could it be a lens of criticism, fighting to be right, pride, thinking you're not good enough or loved, not talented, etc. Pay attention to how you feel and then focus on the thought that came right before that.)

Imagine: The negative thought/feeling is like a pair of dark lenses you're looking through. Say to your higher power, "Please take this lens of (fill in the blank: doubt, fear, judgment, shame, etc.), I choose instead to look through a lens of (fill in the blank: love, forgiveness, gratitude, etc.).

I choose to look through a lens of _____

Step 2—Listen:
Sit quietly and breathe deeply from your belly for a few minutes, as you allow your thoughts to flow.

Ponder: What is tugging at my heart and mind to do, say, or learn more about today?

_____

_____

_____

_____

LIST your thoughts above, or in a separate journal, and then put any action items on your schedule or calendar, with a specific time to accomplish them.

Step 3—Take action:
Are your action items on the calendar? Now consider if you're looking through a negative lens about taking action on this. If so, repeat step 1 and change your lens again!

Remember: Action is the most difficult, yet most transformational, part of this process. Even when you can't see how an action item will help you accomplish your goals, remember that action brings clarity, so it's time to trust the process, change your lens again if needed, and then go for it! Real progress only happens when you take action.

EVENING ACCOUNTABILITY:

What went well today?

_____

_____

What is one thing I can do to prepare for tomorrow?

_____

_____

What were the results of taking action today?

_____

_____

What follow-up item(s) became clear to me after taking action? (put them on your calendar)

_____

_____

Do I need to change my lens, as I think through any of these follow-up action items, and put any of them back on the calendar?

_____

_____

What were results of not taking action today?

_____

_____

Which lens was I looking through that prevented me from taking action?

_____

_____

Who can I share my results with and be accountable to?

_____

_____

What insight was gained by reaching out to that person for accountability?

_____

_____

If I were talking to my best friend, what would I say about the choices made if it were their day I were evaluating?

_____

_____

Two things I'm grateful for are:

_____

_____

One thing I look forward to is:

_____

DAY 26: EXTERNAL/ INTERNAL CRITICS

Never let the external critics become your internal critics.

MORNING MOMENTS

Step 1 - Change your lens:

Ponder: Which negative lens is fighting for my focus?

_____

_____

(Examples: If I feel fearful or anxious about something, am I looking through a lens of doubt, fear, or judgment? Could it be a lens of criticism, fighting to be right, pride, thinking you're not good enough or loved, not talented, etc. Pay attention to how you feel and then focus on the thought that came right before that.)

Imagine: The negative thought/feeling is like a pair of dark lenses you're looking through. Say to your higher power, "Please take this lens of (fill in the blank: doubt, fear, judgment, shame, etc.), I choose instead to look through a lens of (fill in the blank: love, forgiveness, gratitude, etc.).

I choose to look through a lens of _____

Step 2—Listen:

Sit quietly and breathe deeply from your belly for a few minutes, as you allow your thoughts to flow.

> Ponder: What is tugging at my heart and mind to do, say, or learn more about today?
>
> _____
>
> _____
>
> _____
>
> _____

LIST your thoughts above, or in a separate journal, and then put any action items on your schedule or calendar, with a specific time to accomplish them.

Step 3—Take action:

Are your action items on the calendar? Now consider if you're looking through a negative lens about taking action on this. If so, repeat step 1 and change your lens again!

> Remember: Action is the most difficult, yet most transformational, part of this process. Even when you can't see how an action item will help you accomplish your goals, remember that action brings clarity, so it's time to trust the process, change your lens again if needed, and then go for it! Real progress only happens when you take action.

EVENING ACCOUNTABILITY:

What went well today?

_____

_____

What is one thing I can do to prepare for tomorrow?

_____

_____

What were the results of taking action today?

_____

_____

What follow-up item(s) became clear to me after
taking action? (put them on your calendar)

_____

_____

Do I need to change my lens, as I think through any of
these follow-up action items, and put any of them back
on the calendar?

_____

_____

What were results of not taking action today?

_____

_____

Which lens was I looking through that prevented me from taking action?

_____

_____

Who can I share my results with and be accountable to?

_____

_____

What insight was gained by reaching out to that person for accountability?

_____

_____

If I were talking to my best friend, what would I say about the choices made if it were their day I were evaluating?

_____

_____

Two things I'm grateful for are:

_____

_____

One thing I look forward to is:

_____

DAY 27: PROGRESS NOT PERFECTION

Life is not about perfection,
it's about progression.
It's about trying again
and again and again.

It's about standing up one
more time than you fall.

MORNING MOMENTS

Step 1- Change your lens:

Ponder: Which negative lens is fighting for my focus?

_____

_____

(Examples: If I feel fearful or anxious about something, am I looking through a lens of doubt, fear, or judgment? Could it be a lens of criticism, fighting to be right, pride, thinking you're not good enough or loved, not talented, etc. Pay attention to how you feel and then focus on the thought that came right before that.)

Imagine: The negative thought/feeling is like a pair of dark lenses you're looking through. Say to your higher power, "Please take this lens of (fill in the blank: doubt, fear, judgment, shame, etc.), I choose instead to look through a lens of (fill in the blank: love, forgiveness, gratitude, etc.).

I choose to look through a lens of _____

Step 2—Listen:

Sit quietly and breathe deeply from your belly for a few minutes, as you allow your thoughts to flow.

Ponder: What is tugging at my heart and mind to do, say, or learn more about today?

_____

_____

_____

_____

LIST your thoughts above, or in a separate journal, and then put any action items on your schedule or calendar, with a specific time to accomplish them.

Step 3—Take action:

Are your action items on the calendar? Now consider if you're looking through a negative lens about taking action on this. If so, repeat step 1 and change your lens again!

Remember: Action is the most difficult, yet most transformational, part of this process. Even when you can't see how an action item will help you accomplish your goals, remember that action brings clarity, so it's time to trust the process, change your lens again if needed, and then go for it! Real progress only happens when you take action.

EVENING ACCOUNTABILITY:

What went well today?

_____

_____

What is one thing I can do to prepare for tomorrow?

_____

_____

What were the results of taking action today?

_____

_____

What follow-up item(s) became clear to me after taking action? (put them on your calendar)

_____

_____

Do I need to change my lens, as I think through any of these follow-up action items, and put any of them back on the calendar?

_____

_____

What were results of not taking action today?

_____

_____

Which lens was I looking through that prevented me from taking action?

_____

_____

Who can I share my results with and be accountable to?

_____

_____

What insight was gained by reaching out to that person for accountability?

_____

_____

If I were talking to my best friend, what would I say about the choices made if it were their day I were evaluating?

_____

_____

Two things I'm grateful for are:

_____

_____

One thing I look forward to is:

_____

DAY 28: STRUGGLES UNVEIL OUR STRENGTHS

Struggles unveil strengths.

Keep going! Your
strength is growing!

MORNING MOMENTS

Step 1–Change your lens:

Ponder: Which negative lens is fighting for my focus?

_____

_____

(Examples: If I feel fearful or anxious about something, am I looking through a lens of doubt, fear, or judgment? Could it be a lens of criticism, fighting to be right, pride, thinking you're not good enough or loved, not talented, etc. Pay attention to how you feel and then focus on the thought that came right before that.)

Imagine: The negative thought/feeling is like a pair of dark lenses you're looking through. Say to your higher power, "Please take this lens of (fill in the blank: doubt, fear, judgment, shame, etc.), I choose instead to look through a lens of (fill in the blank: love, forgiveness, gratitude, etc.).

I choose to look through a lens of _____

Step 2—Listen:

Sit quietly and breathe deeply from your belly for a few minutes, as you allow your thoughts to flow.

> Ponder: What is tugging at my heart and mind to do, say, or learn more about today?
>
> _____
>
> _____
>
> _____
>
> _____

LIST your thoughts above, or in a separate journal, and then put any action items on your schedule or calendar, with a specific time to accomplish them.

Step 3—Take action:

Are your action items on the calendar? Now consider if you're looking through a negative lens about taking action on this. If so, repeat step 1 and change your lens again!

> Remember: Action is the most difficult, yet most transformational, part of this process. Even when you can't see how an action item will help you accomplish your goals, remember that action brings clarity, so it's time to trust the process, change your lens again if needed, and then go for it! Real progress only happens when you take action.

EVENING ACCOUNTABILITY:

What went well today?

_____

_____

What is one thing I can do to prepare for tomorrow?

_____

_____

What were the results of taking action today?

_____

_____

What follow-up item(s) became clear to me after taking action? (put them on your calendar)

_____

_____

Do I need to change my lens, as I think through any of these follow-up action items, and put any of them back on the calendar?

_____

_____

What were results of not taking action today?

_____

_____

Which lens was I looking through that prevented me from taking action?

_____

_____

Who can I share my results with and be accountable to?

_____

_____

What insight was gained by reaching out to that person for accountability?

_____

_____

If I were talking to my best friend, what would I say about the choices made if it were their day I were evaluating?

_____

_____

Two things I'm grateful for are:

_____

_____

One thing I look forward to is:

_____

DAY 29: GOD'S OPINION OF ME MATTERS MOST

God's opinion of me, is the only one that truly counts.

MORNING MOMENTS

Step 1- Change your lens:

Ponder: Which negative lens is fighting for my focus?

_____

_____

(Examples: If I feel fearful or anxious about something, am I looking through a lens of doubt, fear, or judgment? Could it be a lens of criticism, fighting to be right, pride, thinking you're not good enough or loved, not talented, etc. Pay attention to how you feel and then focus on the thought that came right before that.)

Imagine: The negative thought/feeling is like a pair of dark lenses you're looking through. Say to your higher power, "Please take this lens of (fill in the blank: doubt, fear, judgment, shame, etc.), I choose instead to look through a lens of (fill in the blank: love, forgiveness, gratitude, etc.).

I choose to look through a lens of _____

Step 2—Listen:
Sit quietly and breathe deeply from your belly for a few minutes, as you allow your thoughts to flow.

> Ponder: What is tugging at my heart and mind to do, say, or learn more about today?
>
> _____
>
> _____
>
> _____
>
> _____

LIST your thoughts above, or in a separate journal, and then put any action items on your schedule or calendar, with a specific time to accomplish them.

Step 3—Take action:
Are your action items on the calendar? Now consider if you're looking through a negative lens about taking action on this. If so, repeat step 1 and change your lens again!

> Remember: Action is the most difficult, yet most transformational, part of this process. Even when you can't see how an action item will help you accomplish your goals, remember that action brings clarity, so it's time to trust the process, change your lens again if needed, and then go for it! Real progress only happens when you take action.

EVENING ACCOUNTABILITY:

What went well today?

_____

_____

What is one thing I can do to prepare for tomorrow?

_____

_____

What were the results of taking action today?

_____

_____

What follow-up item(s) became clear to me after taking action? (put them on your calendar)

_____

_____

Do I need to change my lens, as I think through any of these follow-up action items, and put any of them back on the calendar?

_____

_____

What were results of not taking action today?

_____

_____

Which lens was I looking through that prevented me from taking action?

_____

_____

Who can I share my results with and be accountable to?

_____

_____

What insight was gained by reaching out to that person for accountability?

_____

_____

If I were talking to my best friend, what would I say about the choices made if it were their day I were evaluating?

_____

_____

Two things I'm grateful for are:

_____

_____

One thing I look forward to is:

_____

DAY 30: CONFIDENCE COMES AFTER ACTION

One year will go by whether you plan for it or not.

It's the small, daily steps that make the biggest difference.

MORNING MOMENTS

Step 1- Change your lens:

Ponder: Which negative lens is fighting for my focus?

_____

_____

(Examples: If I feel fearful or anxious about something, am I looking through a lens of doubt, fear, or judgment? Could it be a lens of criticism, fighting to be right, pride, thinking you're not good enough or loved, not talented, etc. Pay attention to how you feel and then focus on the thought that came right before that.)

Imagine: The negative thought/feeling is like a pair of dark lenses you're looking through. Say to your higher power, "Please take this lens of (fill in the blank: doubt, fear, judgment, shame, etc.), I choose instead to look through a lens of (fill in the blank: love, forgiveness, gratitude, etc.).

I choose to look through a lens of _____

Step 2—Listen:

Sit quietly and breathe deeply from your belly for a few minutes, as you allow your thoughts to flow.

> Ponder: What is tugging at my heart and mind to do, say, or learn more about today?
>
> _____
>
> _____
>
> _____
>
> _____

LIST your thoughts above, or in a separate journal, and then put any action items on your schedule or calendar, with a specific time to accomplish them.

Step 3—Take action:

Are your action items on the calendar? Now consider if you're looking through a negative lens about taking action on this. If so, repeat step 1 and change your lens again!

> Remember: Action is the most difficult, yet most transformational, part of this process. Even when you can't see how an action item will help you accomplish your goals, remember that action brings clarity, so it's time to trust the process, change your lens again if needed, and then go for it! Real progress only happens when you take action.

EVENING ACCOUNTABILITY:

What went well today?

_____

_____

What is one thing I can do to prepare for tomorrow?

_____

_____

What were the results of taking action today?

_____

_____

What follow-up item(s) became clear to me after taking action? (put them on your calendar)

_____

_____

Do I need to change my lens, as I think through any of these follow-up action items, and put any of them back on the calendar?

_____

_____

What were results of not taking action today?

_____

_____

Which lens was I looking through that prevented me from taking action?

_____

_____

Who can I share my results with and be accountable to?

_____

_____

What insight was gained by reaching out to that person for accountability?

_____

_____

If I were talking to my best friend, what would I say about the choices made if it were their day I were evaluating?

_____

_____

Two things I'm grateful for are:

_____

_____

One thing I look forward to is:

_____

Congratulations! You made it! Give yourself a well-deserved pat on the back. How do you feel? What are your thoughts or questions now that you're finished?

_____

_____

_____

_____

It's time to Inspect Your Perspective once again. Remember to sit in a quiet place and jot down the first number that comes to your mind. Don't overthink it; there are no right or wrong answers, just notice them and write them down.

Inspect Your Perspective

Where I am Now   **Where I Want to Be**

0-10	STATEMENT	0-10
	I recognize my emotions as I feel them	
	I can identify when what I'm feeling is a result of what I'm thinking or saying to myself	
	I recognize how my internal dialogue influences the way I feel	

	I feel that I can truly be myself around others	
	I notice whether things are happening to me or within me	
	I recognize the consequences of my thoughts and internal dialog	
	I am an active listener when others speak to me	
	I keep my emotions in check and choose to act instead of react	
	I can easily build rapport with others	
	I can read other's emotions	
	I know how to calm myself down when I feel upset or anxious	
	I invite feedback and ways to improve	
	I pay attention to what my heart and mind are nudging me to do	

	I set long term goals and assess them on a regular basis	
	I am confident in making decisions and taking action on them	
	I feel strong and capable	
	I know how to calm myself when I'm upset or anxious & don't let it derail my whole day	
	I know I have weaknesses and I'm not embarrassed by them	
	I am aware of how I spend my time each day	
	I am aware of my habits	
	I am aware of my expectations	
	I'm aware of how I respond when expectations aren't met	
	I don't expect others to live up to my unspoken expectations, I love them where they are	

	I plan time for fun and relaxation	
	I allow time for reflection in my day	
	I take action daily toward my goals	
	I focus on the lessons in life rather than the losses	
	I keep my emotions in check and don't let them derail my day or week	
	I love myself	
	The words I say to myself are kind, forgiving and loving	
	I don't avoid conflict, I face challenges and look for ways beyond them	
	←-Add each number down the columns and write your answers—>	

Time to compare your scores.

Day 1 score: Where I am ____ where I want to be ____

Day 30 score: Where I am ____ where I want to be ____

Finally, rate your efforts over the past 30 days from 0-10. ____

Remember, there's not shame in this. Just notice your overall efforts and if you'd like to improve them, then pull out a notebook and repeat the process if you need to repeat.

Did you get out of it what you put into it? ____

Conclusion:

So? How did you do? What areas did you improve in and which ones would you like to continue to improve? Now that you have finished this book, I encourage you to continue to use those 3 simple steps daily.

Training the mind to work for you is a continuous process, it's not one and done. I use these steps daily and I encourage you to do that as well.

I'm grateful you have embarked upon this journey with me. I know you have what it takes to create the life you imagine, but it begins with changing your lens, then listening, and then taking action.

Go on and take that leap of faith. You've got this!

Made in the USA
Monee, IL
11 March 2020